Dear Lord, I Can't Do It All!

Dear Lord, I Can't Do It All!

Meditations for Single Mothers

by Bobbie Reed

Publishing House
St. Louis

Copyright © 1991 Concordia Publishing House
3558 S. Jefferson Avenue, St. Louis, MO 63118-3968
Manufactured in the United States of America.

Library of Congress Cataloging-in-Publication Data
Reed, Bobbie.
    Dear Lord, I can't do it all : meditations for single mothers/ by Bobbie Reed.
       p.   cm.
    ISBN 0-570-04199-6
    1. Single mothers—Prayer-books and devotions—English.
  I. Title.
  BV4596.S48R44   1991
242′.6431—dc20   90-45570
                                             CIP

1 2 3 4 5 6 7 8 9 10 PB 00 99 98 97 96 95 94 93 92 91

To Yvonne Karlin, with love, another single parent who not only survived, but came through with increased faith, a joyous spirit, and a loving heart.

CONTENTS

FEELINGS

SPECIAL DAYS

MY EX AND OTHER PEOPLE

THE KIDS

CHALLENGES

HOPE

JOY

Feelings

1. I FEEL LONELY

I feel lonely, Lord. It's hard to be a single mom. Sometimes I feel as if I'd like to be a child again, and climb up on Daddy's lap and be cuddled, all safe and protected. Sometimes I miss being married. I want to be held, and loved, and made love to. I miss the closeness, the tenderness, and the warmth of being married.

I get up in the mornings and have no one with whom to share my plans for the day. The kids don't really care that I have an important meeting at work that I'm dreading. I want someone to talk with.

It seems that some days are more lonely than others. At times the loneliness is just a mild sense of someone missing from my life. But on occasion, like today, the pain starts deep inside my empty heart and spreads to mess up my thinking. Today, it seemed that everyone else in the world was a couple. There were two people—a man and a woman—in most of the cars I passed on the freeway. Even in the parking lot, couples were walking to the office together. Everywhere I looked, people seemed to have found partners. I felt rejected and neglected. Today I feel as if I'm never going to be loved again. I am almost convinced that everyone I'll ever care about will walk out on me, and leave me lonelier than ever.

Then, right in the middle of my loneliness, I seemed to hear You whisper reassuringly, firmly, "I'm here. I'll never leave you nor forsake you." And I realized that I am never truly alone. You are with me. You genuinely care about my every thought, decision, challenge, and choice. You know me completely and love me still. You are the best friend I'll ever have; the only One I can truly count on to always be there for me.

When I experience loneliness and let it lead to self pity,

I think I'm forgetting that You are there. Oh, Lord, do You feel neglected, ignored, overlooked, and even lonely sometimes when I forget You?

I'm sorry, Lord. I'm glad You're with me. I'll try to be a better friend.

I love You.

> . . . He Himself has said, 'I will never desert you, nor will I ever forsake you,' so that we confidently say, 'The Lord is my helper, I will not be afraid. What shall man do to me?' (Heb. 13:5–6).

2. I FEEL OVERWHELMED BY ALL I HAVE TO DO

I had to get up pretty early this morning, Lord. I had so much to do. When you're a single mom, you have to do the work of two people! Oh, the kids can help some, and some chores get little more than a lick and a promise, but there's still plenty left over to do.

There's the cooking, the cleaning, the mending, the yard, the laundry, the shopping, the car repairs to arrange, driving the kids everywhere, the innumerable errands, and a thousand other little jobs that never seem to get done. I'm suffering from *task overload*!

Then, there's the 24-hour responsibility for the finances, the safety of the kids, the disciplining, the encouraging, the teaching, the sharing of spiritual values, and the managing of the home and our family life. It's a lot to be concerned about and, at times, I experience *responsibility overload*!

On top of that, I'm responsible for the emotional stability of our home. Even when I'm upset, feeling lonely or angry, or on those days when I'm in need of affirmation or reassurance, I must be careful to provide love, affirmation, understanding, and support for the children. There's no one else here to help balance my own moods. I've got to grow up myself. At times I'm on *emotional overload*!

It's too much to expect of any one person! I guess I'm the one who's putting all these expectations on myself. You don't expect me to do all of this alone, do You? You're there to help me. You send me friends to help, to build me up and support me.

I'll admit there's a certain sense of satisfaction when I've crossed off a lot of things on my "to-do" list. But, I need to learn to be more realistic in my expectations.

Help me evaluate my lists, Lord, and choose the tasks I genuinely need to do. Give me the discernment to see creative ways to combine or eliminate less important chores. Teach me to stop *running* so fast and to learn to *walk* my life. I need to slow down and find the joy in life. Maybe if I do this, the kids and I will actually have a better relationship. If I risk being a human being with feelings of my own with my children, instead of trying to be only a tower of strength, maybe they will learn how to better handle negative feelings they may have.

It's a different approach, Lord. Help me try. Strengthen me to the task.

> He gives strength to the weary, and to him who lacks might He increases power. Though youths grow weary and tired, and vigorous young men stumble badly, yet those who wait for the Lord will gain new strength; They will mount up with wings like eagles, they will run and not get tired, they will walk and not become weary (Is. 40:29–31).

3. I'M GLAD JUST TO BE ALIVE

Life is wonderful, Lord. This morning I woke up refreshed and eager to start the day. It's fun to realize that the hours stretched out ahead are waiting for me to fill them. (Not that there's ever any problem filling up the time—actually I could use a few extra hours every day!)

Last night's rain had washed the sky, leaving it as blue as I've ever seen it. The flowers in the garden are like bright appliques on the blanket of green grass. And the birds' songs are clear and sweet. I guess I'm waxing poetic, but that's how I feel today, just as if everything is new and fresh.

Today I resolved to be a better mother, to take time to not only listen to and provide for the children, but to also enjoy them. I decided to show them love by making their favorite dinner tonight and playing games together afterwards. So often I'm too busy or too tired to do that. Today, we really had fun together.

This morning I resolved to be a better neighbor and spend a few of my precious minutes talking with and listening to old Mrs. Schorner next door. So often I just smile and wave at her. Today I did more.

Today I resolved to be a better daughter to You, Lord, and also spend more time with You. It seems so often I rush through my prayers and my Bible reading, almost as if You weren't there. Today You and I genuinely communed together.

Today I'm filled with such a sense of inner joy. My step is lighter, and I feel like skipping instead of walking. I find I'm smiling without even trying to, and I keep singing little snatches of my favorite songs.

Today is one of those perfect days which I'd like to

repeat and repeat forever. It's easy to rejoice in Your goodness when I feel so excited just to be alive.

Hope You had a good day, too, Lord.

> What we have seen and heard we proclaim to you also, that you also may have fellowship with us; and indeed our fellowship is with the Father, and with His Son Jesus Christ. And these things we write, so that our joy may be made complete (1 John 1:3–4).
> . . . I came that they might have life, and might have it abundantly (John 10:10).

4. MY FEELINGS ARE HURT

I'm hurt, Lord. Today my oldest child yelled at me, "I hate you!" and my feelings are really hurt. What awful words. Even though I know in my heart that my child's feelings of anger are short lived and that he doesn't truly hate me, it is hard to hear those words.

He wanted to build a high ramp out of boards and jump his bicycle off of it. The boards were too flimsy and his riding skills not up to such ambitious (and unsafe) feats. I put my foot down and said, "no." He couldn't understand why and claimed that I never let him have any fun and that we could never afford to do good things like some of his friends.

It's true the dollars are stretched pretty thinly at times, but Lord, You know how hard I work at planning fun things for the kids. I've worked overtime to have the money for their bikes. It is so unfair for a child to say such things, especially "I hate you."

I would never have dared say something like that to my parents! And yet, if I'm honest, I did on occasion as a child have feelings of anger and dislike toward them. I just didn't voice those feelings aloud. I guess children will always have times when they are frustrated with their parents.

I suppose I want my kids to somehow understand that even if they don't like my decisions, I am making them because I love them. That's a lot to expect of children. It's probably a lot to expect of myself, too, because I guess I'm sometimes upset with You when You don't give me what I want. You want what is best for me. I need to trust You more.

Somehow, whenever I come to You with my anger, my hurt feelings, or other pain, You always seem to help me see the broader picture, and You comfort me. Thanks, Lord.

> Blessed be the God and Father of our Lord Jesus Christ, the Father of mercies and God of all comfort; who comforts us in all our affliction so that we may be able to comfort those who are in any affliction with the comfort with which we ourselves are comforted by God (2 Cor. 1:3–4).

5. I'M SO TIRED I COULD SLEEP FOR A WEEK

I've started having fantasies about sleeping, Lord. My idea of a perfect vacation right now is a hotel room with no telephone and no kids, and not telling anyone where I am for at least three days. I wouldn't even eat—just sleep, sleep, and sleep!

I know why I'm tired, but I'm not sure what to do

about it. I've had to be creative with my schedule since becoming a single mom. I get up an hour early so I can do a load of laundry each morning before work. I've found that I can do a lot of chores in the evenings after the kids are asleep. That way I can spend the early evenings with them, supervising homework, playing games, talking, and loving. Weekends are filled with their ball games and music lessons, as well as at least one fun activity and a few chores. Keeping up this schedule means less sleep for me. I guess it's all catching up with me.

I think You understand, Lord. You said that all of us who were weary could come to You and find rest. Sounds wonderful!

Maybe I could wash only three days a week and catch an extra hour's rest at least two days a week. Maybe there are some ways to get the chores done earlier in the evenings without infringing on my time with the kids. Maybe I can take this Saturday and sleep a few hours. I'll try.

Even though my body is tired, my spirit is strong, and I have a little song in my heart because You are my Lord. You share the parenting role for my children. You care about their well-being probably even more than I do, if that's possible. It's great to know that we're doing okay together, the kids and You and I.

Continue to refresh my spirit, and I'll try to get some rest for my body.

> Come to Me, all who are weary and heavy-laden, and I will give you rest. Take My yoke upon you, and learn from Me, for I am gentle and humble in heart; and you shall find rest for your souls (Matt. 11:28–29).

6. I NEED A HUG!

When I woke up this morning I knew I needed a hug. Remember my prayer, I told You I needed a hug. And I got not just one hug, but several today.

That's because I've learned how to handle these kind of days. I go after hugs! The first thing this morning at work I went over to one of my friends and announced that I wanted a hug. Immediately she jumped up and hugged me. (I do the same for her on her needy days.) There's nothing quite like warm bear hugs from friends. Hugs say they care. A hug makes the world seem a safe place. A hug stops the whirl for a brief moment. I love hugs.

Then on my break, I called my mother and told her I needed a hug. She gave me "verbal hugs" as she listened to my woes and we ended up laughing together. I hung up feeling hugged.

I lunched with a friend who is going through a divorce. She's really hurting, and I was able to comfort her because of my own experience of losing a relationship. I held her close for a brief hug and she clung to me, hugging me back. (I've learned that whenever I give a hug, I usually get one back!)

Then after supper, while the kids were watching a video, I made a list of all the ways You show me that You love me. The list was quite long. Some of the really important ways are:

• You keep my children safe each day.
• You provide a good job for me.
• We are all healthy.
• You give me terrific friends.
• You've given our pastor a real understanding of the challenges of being a single parent, so he is helpful to me.
• You paint beautiful sunrises and sunsets.

• You gave me a parking place up front of the parking lot this morning when I had a lot of boxes to take into the office.

• When I needed $52.15 for car repairs, You sent me a refund on an overpayment I'd made of which I was unaware. Lord, thanks for hugging me.

> Beloved, let us love one another, for love is from God; and everyone who loves is born of God and knows God. The one who does not love does not know God, for God is love. By this the love of God was manifested in us, that God has sent His only begotten Son into the world so that we might live through Him. In this is love, not that we loved God, but that He loved us and sent His Son to be the propitiation for our sins. Beloved, if God so loved us, we also ought to love one another (1 John 4:7–11).

7. I COULD USE A GOOD LAUGH

What makes You laugh, Lord? I know You laugh at some of our foolishness, but what would make You laugh with joy? I love to laugh, although sometimes I sense just a touch of hysteria in my giggles.

When I laugh I sense my tensions easing away and I begin to relax. A good laugh has got to be the equivalent of a 30-minute break, a ten-minute nap, or a three-minute neck rub! When I laugh I am more *human* than *mother*, with a capital "M."

I've laughed at puppies tumbling over one another to get to their mother. Or at the kitten when he got tangled up in a ball of string. He had such an astonished look on his face! I laughed with the children last night when they got together and put on a "play" they had written. It was hilarious and very creative.

Sometimes, after the fact, I laugh at myself because I got so uptight and worried about something that never even happened.

I do laugh. But on the whole, I don't actually laugh enough. I want to develop a lifestyle that is confident in Your ability to ensure that all things work together for my good. I want laughter to be more natural than worry or fear. I want to truly rejoice in the secure knowledge of Your love.

I've found that laughter helps me get through the tough times. If I can find something ridiculous, or at least humorous, in the situation, I can begin to rise above the negative feelings. Help me, Lord, to learn to laugh more easily than I do now.

> Rejoice in the Lord always; again I will say, rejoice! (Phil. 4:4).
> A joyful heart is good medicine (Prov. 17:22).

8. WILL I EVER GET WHAT I LONG FOR?

Sometimes I'm ready to give up hope, Lord! I want so many things for our family, and sometimes it seems none of them will come to pass.

I want my children to develop a real relationship with You, bringing their own prayer requests to You, and spontaneously praising You for the good things You bring into their lives. Last week I saw real progress when my oldest commented that we should thank God because we made it to a gas station without running out of gas. And we did, remember? We bowed our heads right there in the Chevron station and thanked You. But then this morning I felt discouraged because both kids didn't want to go to Sunday school. How do I teach them to love going to Your house?

I want my children to learn to show love to other people, to share whatever You give to us, and to be willing to do things for others. Last month we all went next door and helped the neighbor with her yard work. She can't do as much as she used to and she appreciated it so. The kids felt good about helping that day. But I can't succeed in teaching them to share their things, and very often I end up having to referee arguments over toys.

I want my children to grow up with good decision-making skills. I try to give them choices to make each day, so they can practice making decisions and living with the consequences. Sometimes they do okay, but all too often they don't make wise choices. Will they ever learn?

Maybe I'm just too impatient and I want too much to happen all at once. I do have to admit that the kids are making progress in almost all of the areas I'm hoping for. I need to stop pushing so hard and focusing on what I want, and place my hope in You. I'll commit to do my best as teacher, as model, and as mom, and I'll commit the kids and their growth into Your hands.

Look after my family, Lord.

Hope deferred makes the heart sick, but desire fulfilled is a tree of life (Prov. 13:12).

For in hope we have been saved, but hope that is seen is not hope; for why does one also hope for what he sees? But if we hope for what we do not see, with perseverance we wait eagerly for it (Rom. 8:24–25).

9. I WON'T WORRY ABOUT TOMORROW

Thank You for today, Lord. I got out the bills, even the unexpected ones, and somehow my paycheck covered them all. I was afraid I'd be short, but I wasn't.

However, there was so little left over that I wasn't sure how we were going to make it through the week. I started to get worried about what would happen if the car broke down, or if the full gas tank didn't last until next payday. As I thought about these things, a dozen other worries came to mind. What if one of the kids became ill? What if the plumbing backed up again? What if more bills came in? Soon, I discovered I was tense and my stomach was in knots.

Then, ever so gently, Your Spirit quieted me, reminding me that You had not only taken care of us today, but every day of our lives, especially since we've been a one-parent family. Even though there have been tough times, we have never been left alone. You have worked lots of little miracles in our lives. You've sent us groceries from unexpected sources. You've provided tires for the car when we couldn't afford them. You've protected us from serious illnesses. Yes, Lord, You do take good care of us.

So, I decided right then and there to just let go of my fears and not to worry about the "what if's" tomorrow might bring. Instead, I would trust in You to handle the future.

I wonder why trusting You isn't easier than it is. Over and over You've proven Your faithfulness, and yet I still catch myself being afraid You won't come through. I think this week, no, this month, I'm going to really work on building my trust in You. Whenever I start to tense up, whatever the reason, I'm going to stop and remind myself that I'm trusting You to work things out the best way.

With practice, and with Your loving promises, I'm going to learn to not worry about tomorrow!

> Be anxious for nothing, but in everything by prayer and supplication with thanksgiving let your requests be made known to God. And the peace of God, which surpasses all comprehension, shall guard your hearts and your minds in Christ Jesus. Finally, brethren, whatever is true, whatever is honorable, whatever is right, whatever is pure, whatever is lovely, whatever is of good repute, if there is any excellence and if anything worthy of praise, let your mind dwell on these things. The things you have learned and received and heard and seen in me, practice these things; and the God of peace shall be with you (Phil. 4:6–9).

10. I'M GLAD YOU MADE BEAUTIFUL SUNRISES

You have such an eye for beauty, Lord. Sometimes I am amazed at the detail of Your handiwork. Tiny, perfect wild flowers. Adorable puppies with soft brown eyes. Fluffy, fleecy clouds set in a brilliant expanse of blue sky. And the sunsets, and gorgeous sunrises.

With all You have to be concerned with, how did You find the time to create our world with so many little perfect touches of beauty? You could have made just one kind of flower and one kind of tree with leaves all the same. Snowflakes could all be alike for all the notice some of us take of them. And yet, You did take the time to create a beautiful world for us.

When I walk on the beach or in the woods, I am so aware that the beauty in nature is Your handiwork. I feel as if I'm learning more about You by taking the time to appreciate what You've made. I like praying out-of-doors because among the flowers, the trees, and near the water, I somehow feel closer to You.

Teach me to stop more often and notice the messages You send by Your handiwork. There is a sense of expansive peace proclaimed in each majestic sunset that seems to quiet my soul and convince me that the worst is over. There is a message of joyous hope for a brand new day in each morning sunrise that speaks to my heart, calling it to awaken confident in Your power. As the light changes and the sun rises, I am energized with Your messages of love.

Thank You, Lord, for sunrises.

> The heavens are telling of the glory of God; and their expanse is declaring the work of His hands. Day to day pours forth speech, and night to night reveals knowledge. There is no speech, nor are there words; their voice is not heard. Their line has gone out through all the earth, and their utterances to the end of the world. . . . Let the words of my mouth and the meditation of my heart be acceptable in Thy sight, O Lord, my rock and my Redeemer (Ps. 19:1–4, 14).

11. TODAY I FEEL LIKE A FAILURE

I really blew it today, Lord. The kids came in earlier than usual after school and caught me gossiping with a friend. We weren't being very nice. And after listening for a while, one of the kids said accusingly, "You always tell us not to talk mean about people, so how come you do it?"

What could I say? It's hard being caught by my own child violating the very values I've been trying to teach them. I was so depressed, and I felt I'd undone perhaps months' worth of progress in that area with the kids.

I know that just telling kids what to do is not effective in communicating values unless I also live by those same values. I must model them if I expect my kids to even consider the values I expound.

You were such a perfect model of what You sought to teach us. Your patience with those who questioned You and sought to trap You. Your kindness to all those who needed You every time You turned around. Your tenderness toward the children. Your wisdom when teaching. Your taking time out to be alone and to pray. In so many ways You modeled the lifestyle You wanted us to develop.

I want to be a better model to my children. That means I must make a few changes in my behavior, not only when they are around, but even when I don't think they can see or hear me. I've got to be more consistent in my walk with You.

Help me become aware of and correct the inconsistencies.

> For this reason also, since the day we heard of it, we have not ceased to pray for you and to ask that you may be filled with the knowledge of His will in all spiritual wisdom and understanding, so that you may walk in a manner worthy of the Lord, to please Him in all respects, bearing fruit in every good work and increasing in the knowledge of God; strengthened with all power, according to His glorious might, for the attaining of all steadfastness and patience; joyously giving thanks to the Father, who has qualified us to share in the inheritance of the saints in light (Col. 1:9–12).

12. I'M AT THE END OF MY ROPE

Is today finally over, Lord? I hope so. I can't take any more. I've really reached the limits of my endurance. Everything went wrong today. I've tried to be strong and to take care of everything, but things don't seem to be cooperating, especially today.

The school principal called, asking that I come in to discuss my son's misbehavior. The plumber called to say the little repair job is now going to be a major repair job. And my cold (or flu) seems to be hanging on forever.

Lord, I've tried so hard to teach my children the right way to behave, why won't they obey the rules? And how are we ever going to pay for the repairs to the house? I do wish I felt better; it's hard to be strong when I'm sick. I just feel that if one more thing goes wrong, I'm going to lose my mind!

But every time I get to this point, You remind me ever so firmly, ever so gently, that You're with me and that I am not alone. I can turn to You and know that You will provide wisdom, resources, and strength. You never fail me or abandon me, even when I get near the end of my rope and start unraveling a bit around the ends. Your Holy Spirit urges me to trust You more, to let You work out the things over which I have no control. And when I listen and begin to trust You more, I find that I don't need to hang on to my rope (or my sanity) as tightly, for I am being held in Your arms and in Your hands.

And so the crisis passes.

> For all things are for your sakes, that the grace which is spreading to more and more people may cause the giving of thanks to abound to the glory of God.

Therefore we do not lose heart, but though our outer, man is decaying, yet our inner man is being renewed day by day. For momentary, light affliction is producing for us an eternal weight of glory far beyond all comparison, while we look not at the things which are seen, but at the things which are not seen; for the things which are seen are temporal, but the things which are not seen are eternal (2 Cor. 4:15–18).

13. SOME DAYS ARE SO FRUSTRATING

I know You were watching, Lord, when I threw that cup across the kitchen and broke it into a thousand tiny pieces. Did You smile at my childishness, knowing that I was creating one more mess to clean up? It's okay, I was a little amused at myself! But mostly, I was frustrated.

I needed to get to work a half an hour early this morning and, of course, everything went wrong. There was a spot on the front of the white suit I'd planned to wear. That suit was perfect for my interview today for a possible promotion. Nothing else in my closet was as nice. I had to wear another outfit and I felt ugly. My hair wouldn't cooperate and I broke a fingernail, all before breakfast. I was grumbling aloud by the time I got to the kitchen. Not only would I not get to work early, at the rate I was going, I'd be late!

The kids spilt the last of the milk, so all there was to feed them was toast and dry (no pun intended) cereal for breakfast. Their arguing over whose fault it was gave me a headache. I yelled at them to shut up and eat. After they left for school, I slipped taking the dishes to the sink and both cereal bowls fell out of my hands and broke, making a lovely mess. There I sat on the floor holding my coffee cup, and suddenly I raised my hand and threw the cup across the room.

I'll confess that it actually felt good!

I know I'd have yelled at the kids if they had reacted that way and deliberately broken something. I'd have made them clean it up and probably pay for the cup. Well, I cleaned up the mess and I'll pay for a new cup, as well as new bowls.

But I wonder how I got to the point of such frustration that I threw a two-year-old-style tantrum? I think it all started when I began worrying about the promotion interview. I guess I forgot that You were in control and that You don't depend on what I wear to work for Your will to be accomplished in my life. If I've been faithful and done my job well, if I've prepared for promotion, my part is done. The rest is in Your hands. And I need to remember that my desired schedule of events may not be the same as Yours. If I trust in Your sovereignty, I can relax and not be so frustrated by the adverse events of the day.

Lord, help me learn to trust You and to have proper priorities so I won't get so frustrated. I have to, Lord. I can't afford to keep buying new cups!

> Do all things without grumbling or disputing; that you may prove yourselves to be blameless and innocent, children of God above reproach in the midst of a crooked and perverse generation, among whom you appear as lights in the world, holding fast the word of life, so that in the day of Christ I may have cause to glory because I did not run in vain nor toil in vain (Phil. 2:14–16).

14. WE ALL SEEMED SO ANGRY TODAY

What a terrible day, Lord. I'm not sure what happened, but we were all angry and ugly with each other. How can we say such hurtful things to people we love?

I am glad no one was listening. But You were listening, weren't You? I guess You're ashamed of us, huh? It's so hard to keep a cool head when someone is yelling mean things at you. At first I was just trying to stop the children's fight, but soon, they were angry with me and the next thing I knew, we were all behaving like two-year-olds!

I've studied better ways to communicate with children and how to avoid power struggles, but no matter how hard I try, I find that my tongue sometimes gets away from me and I say things for which I end up apologizing. At least, I've learned to model that part! I've had a lot of practice.

I genuinely want us to be less ready to be angry with one another. Sometimes it seems the anger is always there, just below the surface, ready to erupt at any time.

Maybe we are all expecting too much of each other. Maybe we need to be more patient, more accepting, and more understanding. I'll have to take the lead, I'm the parent. But I'm going to need Your help.

I've noticed that You never yell at me! Even when I come to You angry or resentful that things aren't going my way, You never yell back at me. You listen, and in a very quiet way, Your Spirit speaks to mine.

I want to be more like You.

A gentle answer turns away wrath, but a harsh word stirs up anger (Prov. 15:1).
Be angry, and yet do not sin; do not let the sun go down on your anger (Eph. 4:26).

Special Days

15. I ENJOYED MOTHER'S DAY

What a special day, Lord. I felt so proud to be a mother today. The kids prepared breakfast for me and even cleaned up the kitchen. They made cards for me at school, and they looked so cute when they brought them in to me. All day they treated me like a queen, and I felt very special.

It's fun once in a while to take a break from being the constant giver to being a receiver. I had to keep reminding myself that today they were being "givers," and to keep stopping myself from stepping in and doing things for them.

Today's sermon was wonderful and I appreciated the pastor's sensitivity to us single mothers. He made a point of recognizing us separately. He said he knew our struggles were hard and said that he honored and respected us. Wow! That felt good. Sometimes I've wondered if he even knew we existed.

A group of us single moms got together for lunch today with our kids, and we went around the table saying what we appreciated most about each other (kids and adults). It was surprising to hear what different people saw and liked in me. I felt strengthened, encouraged, affirmed, and motivated to become better.

Tonight when I tucked the kids in, they hugged me and whispered "I love you." One said, "I'm glad you're my mom!"

Me too, Lord. Me too.

> Her children rise up and bless her (Prov. 31:28).
> Honor your father and your mother, as the Lord your God has commanded you, that your days may be prolonged, and that it may go well with you on the land which the Lord your God gives you (Deut. 5:16).

16. I FOUND FATHER'S DAY HARD

Today was not easy, Lord. It was Father's Day, and all day the kids missed having their father here with us as a family. In a way, I missed it too. I did what I could. The kids bought a gift and we mailed it off to their dad along with their cards. They called him this afternoon, but that only seemed to make them feel even more lonely for him. At lunch, they started telling their favorite "daddy story" and ended up laughing a lot as we remembered the good times we did have.

I tried to distract their attention with various activities and it helped for a while. But by bedtime, I was exhausted with the strain.

I know You've promised to be a father to the fatherless. I've tried to teach the kids that since their dad doesn't live here anymore, they need to turn to You for what they need. But I don't think they actually understand what I mean.

I have noticed, however, that You have provided for the kids in special ways, bringing in needed money for school clothes or bags of groceries when the budget ran out. You have taken over the role of provider. I am sure that You've assigned extra angels to care for the children now that they only have one parent to take care of them. That must be true, for I'm amazed at how they've survived some of their daring acrobatics with their bikes and skateboards. (Forbidden acrobatics, I might note.) You have taken the teaching role and brought various father figures into their lives to help them learn things I cannot teach them. When they do wrong, I sometimes see Your Spirit discipline them and bring them to repentance. And I've seen your love for them ease the path and bring us little surprises.

What a wonderful father You are.

> Sing to God, sing praises to His name; Cast up a highway for Him who rides through the deserts, whose name is the Lord, and exult before Him. A father of the fatherless . . . (Ps. 68:4–5).

17. MY BIRTHDAY ISN'T THE SAME

Did You remember that my birthday is coming up next month, Lord? Birthdays used to be days of celebrating the fact that I was born. My parents used to plan parties for me when I was young. My husband used to give me presents when I was married. Now, no one remembers my birthday unless I mark it on the calendar, and birthdays just mean I'm another year older and still alone.

I've tried baking my own birthday cake and it's just not the same! It's more fun when someone does it for you.

Enough of self pity!

I still get presents—from You. Wonderful presents like my health, my job, my kids, and daily little reminders that You are looking out after me and love me. I am still special to You. You care for me and when I'm sad, it makes You sad to realize that I'm choosing to wallow in despair, instead of trusting in Your love. When I'm happy, I am sure You smile just as I do when I see my kids happy.

I am not alone. You are constantly with me and have promised You will never leave me.

I may be older, but that just means one more year of experiencing Your mercy and Your grace. One more year to have grown more like You.

Yes, enough of self pity.

My birthday is still a month away and I am going to make it special. I can plan a fancy dinner party where we all dress up and behave ever so properly. Or I can get tickets to go see a play. Or I could even take a special trip to somewhere I've always wanted to go. There are a dozen possibilities. I'm actually getting excited. This year my birthday won't be the same—it will be fabulously different and better than ever!

> Every good thing bestowed and every perfect gift
> is from above, coming down from the Father of lights,
> with whom there is no variation, or shifting shadow
> (James 1:17).

18. I DON'T LIKE SPENDING HOLIDAYS ALONE

Holidays aren't much fun these days, Lord. When I was married I used to love holidays. I'd spend a lot of time planning little surprises for the kids, preparing special menus, and decorating the house. My husband used to share in the work and the fun.

Valentine's Day was special for my husband and me. We always took time to express our love in unique ways. For Father's Day, the kids and I would conspire to make their dad's day one to remember, and he and the kids would do the same for me for Mother's Day. He and I used to do our best to give the children very special memories on their birthdays. Holidays always seemed to bring us closer together as a family. Of all the things I miss about the way we used to be, our holiday closeness is up near the top of the list.

Now, holidays are different. I do all the planning either alone or with the kids. There's no husband to share the fun of planning surprises. Sometimes the children don't really care about having holiday menus, preferring hot dogs or hamburgers. I suppose the hardest part is not having the kids on some of the big holidays. They go visit their dad during school breaks, so they're gone for the Fourth of July, Labor Day, Thanksgiving, Christmas, and New Year's Eve.

For us, holiday celebrations have been redefined as we exchange our Christmas gifts early and celebrate some holidays apart.

I'll admit I get a little down in the dumps if I spend holidays alone. So, in the last year, I decided to take charge of holidays. Since I know when the kids will be gone, I plan ways to be with other people on holidays. For the Fourth of July I went to the all-church picnic. On Labor Day I went on a retreat. I had a singles' potluck Thanksgiving dinner at my house, and on Christmas I went to the shelter for the homeless and helped serve meals. New Year's Eve I went to a late communion service at church and then on to a friend's house to spend the night after watching the old year end. We had fun drinking cocoa, talking, and praying together.

It seemed that as I began my plans for each holiday, opportunities opened up for me to be with other people in a variety of ways. It was as if someone had gone along just ahead of me and made special arrangements.

Thanks, Lord. You know how much I hate to be alone on holidays.

> But he who enters by the door is a shepherd of
> the sheep. To him the doorkeeper opens, and the
> sheep hear his voice, and he calls his own sheep by

name, and leads them out. When he puts forth all his own, he goes before them, and the sheep follow him because they know his voice (John 10:2–4).

My Ex and Other People

19. HE DOESN'T TEACH THEM THE SAME VALUES I DO

After the kids came home from visiting their dad this last weekend, they became grouchy and complaining. "Why can't we have a microwave, a videotape recorder, a big screen television, and a new stereo?" they demanded. "Dad has those things!"

Yes, Lord, he does. And neither of us can afford them. He goes ahead and buys what he can't afford and lives one step ahead of the creditors and bankruptcy. I live within my budget, which means doing without some things I'd like to have. And that's not the only value we hold differently. We seem more different than alike, and I'm afraid the kids will choose his values over mine. I know that in the long run, everyone makes an individual choice, and parents cannot decide for their children, but I do so want to!

I want them to grow into mature, Christian adults who are close to You, who are honest, reliable, hardworking, trustworthy, and kind. I want to be proud of them, and I want people to see the best of me in them.

That sounds suspiciously like what You want for me! You want me to become conformed to the image of Christ, to have the fruit of the Spirit in my life, and for people to see You in me. Whoops! I've got some work to do!

I suspect that the more I grow into the woman You want me to be, the better example I'll be to my children. And children learn better by example than by lecture, don't they?

Help me be a good teacher, a good model, and to trust in You to work in their hearts and do the rest.

You are our letter, written in our hearts, known

and read by all men; being manifested that you are a letter of Christ, cared for by us, written not with ink, but with the the Spirit of the living God, not on tablets of stone, but on tablets of human hearts. And such confidence we have through Christ toward God. Not that we are adequate in ourselves to consider anything as coming from ourselves, but our adequacy is from God, who also made us adequate as servants of a new covenant, not of the letter, but of the Spirit; for the letter kills, but the Spirit gives life (2 Cor. 3:2–6).

Humble yourselves, therefore, under the mighty hand of God, . . . casting all your anxiety upon Him, because He cares for you (1 Peter 5:6–7).

20. SOMETIMES MOM CRITICIZES ME AS A PARENT

I know I don't know everything, Lord, but why does Mom sometimes make me feel as if I don't know anything? Today she criticized me for the way I disciplined the kids. They were acting up and being ever so disobedient at the dinner table. I sent them to their rooms before they finished eating.

Mom acted as if I were starving them to death. I don't know if I was right or not, but it seemed appropriate after several warnings and admonitions to them to stop fighting and throwing things at each other.

After Mom went home I started to have doubts. Was I being too harsh? What if they were *really* hungry? Was I being mean?

I've noticed that I often respond to criticism (from anybody) with self-doubts. If someone doesn't like an outfit I'm wearing, I don't wear it again right away, if ever. If someone disagrees with something I say, I'll back down. And if people question my decisions, I usually start to reconsider the issues.

Why am I such a "people pleaser"? I need to seek Your input when making decisions and then stick to what You have led me to do. Other people may have opinions about me and my actions, but the one I truly want to please is You.

Help me be sensitive to Your guidance and to take criticism in stride. Let me hear the feedback from others, but not be so easily swayed or influenced. Help me be pleasing to You.

> For am I now seeking the favor of men, or of God? Or am I striving to please men? If I were still trying to please men, I would not be a bond-servant of Christ (Gal. 1:10).

21. I MISS MY GRANDMOTHER

I remember my grandmother, Lord, with such warm feelings. She used to work so hard, but she always had treats for us kids, home-baked cakes and cookies to snack on. Sometimes I wish she were still around so she could share the moments of joy I have with the kids. A lot of what I try to teach my children I learned from my grandmother. She taught me:
- to do my best at work;
- to take pride in what I do;
- to go to work, even on days when I don't want to;

• to not always speak up and out, to sometimes hold my tongue;

• to enjoy the out-of-doors;

• to be content with what I have, even while striving for more.

Grandmothers are special. Many of my friends tell of learning about You from their grandmothers. Grandmothers give Bible story books to their grandkids and then read to them from those books. Grandmothers teach love and acceptance (while parents are trying to teach love and discipline). Grandmothers make grandkids feel special.

I hope that when the time comes when I will spend time with my own grandkids, I will be one of the best. I want to share my faith. I want to provide genuine love and a sense of being accepting. I want to be the kind of a godly woman who will inspire the grandkids to seek You. A tall order!

Most of all, I'd like to be remembered as the one who taught them about You.

> I thank God, whom I serve with a clear conscience the way my forefathers did, as I constantly remember you in my prayers night and day, longing to see you, even as I recall your tears, so that I may be filled with joy. For I am mindful of the sincere faith within you, which first dwelt in your grandmother Lois, and your mother Eunice, and I am sure that it is in you as well. And for this reason I remind you to kindle afresh the gift of God which is in you through the laying on of my hands. For God has not given us a spirit of timidity, but of power and love and discipline (2 Tim. 1:3–7).

The Kids

22. THE KIDS WERE SO HELPFUL TODAY

Wow! What a day, Lord. We cleaned house from top to bottom, went through the closets and put aside clothes for the Salvation Army truck, washed windows, did the laundry, and straightened out the garage. That may not sound like a lot of work to some people, but You know the mess the house and garage were in!

I'm exhausted. But I'm also happy. The kids helped all day without fighting, without complaining, and without a lot of "horsing around." They were truly helpful! I felt as if we were a team as we scrubbed, dusted, straightened, and sorted. I wish we had more days like this!

I wonder what made the difference between today and the other days? Was it because I included them in planning the day and how we would attack our tasks? Was it because I let them choose the taped music we would play as we moved the tape player from room to room? Was it because I was a little more relaxed than usual and took time to look at some of the things (pictures, books) we unearthed? Was it because we worked together this time rather than my sending them off to do one task while I did another?

I need to figure out what I did right, so I can do it more often. I honestly didn't know the kids could do so well. I think sometimes I let my need to hurry up and get a job done cause me to just do the tasks myself. Instead, I need to continue to let the kids develop skills in working around the house by doing some of the chores. You let me try new things and let me develop my skills in new areas. I'll begin doing that for my kids.

It is by his deeds that a lad distinguishes himself if his conduct is pure and right (Prov. 20:11).

23. I LOVE TO WATCH THE KIDS WHEN THEY'RE SLEEPING

Lord, what is there about sleeping children that is so irresistible? Tonight I slipped into their rooms to make sure they were covered up and warm. I stood for the longest time in the first room, looking at my firstborn. Sleeping children seem to have regained the innocence they had at birth. They look angelic, even with a smear of chocolate for a mustache. I wanted to gather my child close and whisper that no matter what life brought, we would make it as a family. I pulled the blanket up over him and blew him a silent kiss.

I tiptoed into my "baby's" room so I wouldn't wake him. (Wouldn't he hate to know I think of him as my baby?) I couldn't help but smile as I saw his little face buried in his favorite stuffed animal. Awake, he'd never admit still caring for the bear, but asleep, he was vulnerable and open.

Watching them sleep, I am reminded of how much I love them, and somehow a tenderness spreads across my heart, erasing the strain the day has placed on our relationships. Almost, I want to wake them and reassure them that I love them. Almost, but not quite. I'm enjoying the quiet too much!

I said a prayer for each of my children earlier tonight asking Your Holy Spirit to guide them, to bring their lives close to You, and to teach them the ways they should go.

It's a big job, parenting. I need the Holy Spirit to guide me also. Teach us all, Lord.

And thanks for those sleeping moments which remind me of the preciousness of my children.

Now may the God of hope fill you with all joy and peace in believing, that you may abound in hope by the power of the Holy Spirit. And concerning you, my brethren, I myself also am convinced that you yourselves are full of goodness, filled with all knowledge, and able also to admonish one another (Rom. 15:13, 14).

24. I WISH THE KIDS DID BETTER IN SCHOOL

I used to make good grades in school. I loved to learn. I still do. The kids' father continues to go to classes, even today. So how come we have children who seem to care very little about making good grades, behaving in class, or learning anything?

Seems as if every year I find myself sitting in principals' offices or meeting teachers after school to devise ways of motivating better performance from my kids. Both of them are capable, they just don't consider school important.

Sometimes I find myself embarrassed, as if my own value as a person, or at least as a parent, is dependent upon how well my kids perform. I know that's not true. I know in my head, that is, but my stomach doesn't always act as if it agrees. I do want my children to do well for me. I'd feel better if they did. I'd look better to my friends and to my children's teachers. I'd feel more like a success.

But I do also want them to do well for themselves because it will help them be happier and more successful in life. I wish I knew how to convince them of this!

As my parent, I'm sure You're wanting to say, "Listen to yourself!" because You probably have similar thoughts toward me. If I did better in my "school of life," I'd be a better testimony for You and what Your power can do in a yielded life. I'd make You look good to the world. But most of all, I'm sure You want me to do well for myself, for how much better my life could be.

Thank You for forgiving me when I don't live up to Your expectations. Help me be a better student, Lord, so I can be a better teacher.

> I thank my God in all my remembrance of you, always offering prayer with joy in my every prayer for you all, in view of your participation in the Gospel from the first day until now. For I am confident of this very thing, that He who began a good work in you will perfect it until the day of Christ Jesus (Phil. 1:3–6).

25. WE HAD A PROBLEM WITH THE NEIGHBOR AGAIN

What a day, Lord! Last night I discovered that the neighbor's little boy had come over and marked on our front door with an indelible pen. Nothing I used would remove the stains. Even though I was angry, I wrote a carefully worded and gentle note to the parents asking them to repair the door. I had one of the kids take the note over to the neighbor's.

Her response was one of the nastiest letters I've ever read. She accused my kids of every imaginable evil. She called me names. She was vicious and downright mean. Her response was so unfair, considering that I was the one with the damaged front door. Besides, my letter had been very problem-solving-oriented rather than merely accusative.

As You know, I didn't sleep well last night. I kept steaming inside and thinking of ways I could get back at her and repay her meanness.

This morning I wasn't in a very good frame of mind. I kept thinking of getting revenge. It was ruining my day. I knew I wouldn't actually do any of the horrible things I was fantasizing, but I was still furious. Then I remembered the verse about heaping coals of fire on someone's head by being nice. Coals of fire sounded good, so I tried to think of ways to be nice to my neighbor. Suddenly I had a great idea. I picked up the phone and sent her flowers!

As soon as I hung up, I started to giggle. I wished I could see the look on her face when the flowers arrived, and she read the card and saw they were from me! My whole day brightened. I knew that my co-workers would think me crazy to send flowers to someone who had mistreated me, but I got a kick out of the idea. I even laughed aloud a couple of times.

I learned something about anger today, Lord. I don't have to stay angry. I can change my attitude and "get revenge" by being nice. I felt great! (Of course it didn't hurt that her husband came over tonight and repaired my door.)

Thanks for the tip, Lord.

> Never pay back evil for evil to anyone. Respect what is right in the sight of all men. If possible, so far as it depends on you, be at peace with all men. Never take your own revenge, beloved, but leave room for the wrath of God, for it is written, 'Vengeance is mine, I will repay,' says the Lord. But if your enemy is hungry, feed him, and if he is thirsty, give him a drink; for in so doing you will heap burning coals upon his head. Do not be overcome by evil, but overcome evil with good (Rom. 12:17–21).

26. IT HURTS WHEN THE KIDS ARE ANGRY WITH ME

Parenting sure is hard, Lord. Today I was the heavy disciplinarian. I told the kids no party for their friends this weekend, unless all of the chores got done by today. Not only weren't they done, but also the kids wouldn't pitch in and get them done tonight. So, I had them call their friends and cancel the party.

There were pleas, arguments, tears, and finally angry accusations that I never let them do anything. One stormed out of the house and into the garage. The other went to the bedroom and slammed the door. Soon I heard the radio turned up loud. The anger and tension in the house were so strong, I felt I could almost see it. I hate these times.

Doing right. Being consistent. Following through on the rules and consequences I set. That all sounds well and good, but when my children respond with anger, I am so tempted to give in, just to restore the family peace. I don't. I just want to!

I know that it's my job to teach my children not only with words, but also with my actions. I cannot respond to their anger with anger. I need to be firm and fair, and calm. If I can be mature enough to respond correctly, I can be a good teacher and help them learn to deal with difficult situations in a productive way.

You were a good example of giving the proper response. When Judas betrayed You to the Jews, You didn't become angry. You answered quietly, "I am He," to those who sought to capture You. When Martha accused You of not caring about her having to do all of the work, You responded gently that You were aware of her stress, but You didn't give in to what she wanted You to do.

Did you feel badly at those times? I suppose You did.

So, You understand my feelings. Thanks, Lord. Give me courage and strength to do right even when it feels bad.

> And the Lord's bond-servant must not be quarrelsome, but be kind to all, able to teach, patient when wronged, with gentleness correcting those who are in opposition, if perhaps God may grant them repentance leading to the knowledge of the truth, and they may come to their senses and escape from the snare of the devil, having been held captive by him to do his will (2 Tim. 2:24–26).

27. THE KIDS WERE SO LONELY TODAY

I wished for a miracle today, Lord. The kids seemed extra lonely for our lost family today. I would have loved to blink my eyes and take us all back to happier days when we were all together.

Why is it that we don't fully appreciate what we have until we no longer have it? Back in those times (now perceived as happier), we weren't grateful for being an intact family; we just took it for granted. We didn't treat as precious being able to sit around the dinner table and talk together. We weren't always appreciative of having the money to go out to dinner several times a month.

I wonder what things we aren't appreciating enough about what we have now?

• The kids and I have a closer relationship now than we did before.

• There are no more arguments between Mom and Dad in front of the children.

• I get to make the rules, set the discipline, and teach the values I cherish most.

• Our lives are more casual and less regimented now.

• When we do the chores, the kids and I work together.

• The kids keep me from extreme loneliness, and I do the same for them.

• The kids and I do some really fun things like swimming in the river, snowmobile riding, and rollerskating that we never did before.

• I can ensure the kids learn about You and are aware of how much You do for us as a family.

I think I'll plan an appreciation-of-what-we-have activity for the next time the kids have one of these types of days. Thanks for the idea, Lord.

> The Lord raises up those who are bowed down; The Lord loves the righteous; The Lord protects the strangers; He supports the fatherless and the widow (Ps. 146:8b–9a).

28. THE KIDS AND I HAD SO MUCH FUN TODAY

Today was one of those close, loving, and fun days. It was freezing cold outside and raining. The kids couldn't go out, so we built a fire in the fireplace and played a marathon game of Monopoly. We laughed, we gleefully charged each other rent for landing on our properties. We adjourned to the kitchen to work together preparing a huge tray of our favorite snacks. Then back to our game. I felt so close. It was sort of a fantasy-type day like the kind families used to have before television.

We don't do this often, because the kids don't want to miss seeing their favorite television shows, or playing with friends, or doing other things. But sometimes, every so often, we have one of these really special days.

These are days when the kids give me impulsive hugs, when they snuggle close, when they tell me nice things like, "This is fun!" or "I love you, Mom." These days go a long way toward erasing some of the memories of harder days, when running away is so tempting. On good days, I keep telling myself that the kids are feeling as happy and loved as I am. I am sure that deep down they are storing up the good memories and that on bad days, they will remember, at least fleetingly, that there really is a lot of love in our family. I know I do.

I savor those memories, just as I store up the memories of the daily reminders of Your love. The way You show Your love builds up the trust level so that during tough times, when I don't *feel* loved, I can still *know* that You love me.

Help me to never forget Your love.

Who shall separate us from the love of Christ? Shall tribulation, or distress, or persecution, or famine, or nakedness, or peril, or sword? Just as it is written, 'For Thy sake we are being put to death all day long; we were considered as sheep to be slaughtered.' But in all these things we overwhelmingly conquer through Him who loved us. For I am convinced that neither death, nor life, nor angels, nor principalities, nor things present, nor things to come, nor powers, nor height, nor depth, nor any other created thing, shall be able to separate us from the love of God, which is in Christ Jesus our Lord (Rom. 8:35–39).

29. I LEARNED A LOT FROM MY KIDS TODAY

I guess teaching in our family goes both ways, Lord! Today I was the pupil and the kids were the teachers. When I got home from work the little chores I'd left to be done, weren't. The boys were very late coming in for dinner, and I was prepared with lecture number 43. You know, the one about not ever growing up to be reliable if you can't be reliable now. I went over the undone chores, the lateness of the hour, and threw in a few other observations about their unacceptable behaviors.

Suddenly one of the kids looked up at me earnestly and said, "But, Mom, we can't be perfect, we're just very little boys!" It hit me that he was absolutely right.

I was holding them accountable to *always* do the proper things, even though I sometimes leave dishes in the sink overnight or come home late from work. I don't always act the way I should. And I'm not a very little girl. I'm supposed to be grown-up.

I decided to do some reevaluating this evening and see if I've been unrealistic in my expectations. It didn't take long to discover that I had. I need to make some changes.

I wonder if I do the same things to my friends as I have been doing to my children? Do I expect too much? Do I always expect them to do things my way? Am I unforgiving? Am I a bit of a tyrant? I just may be. Boy! Do I need to make some adjustments!

It's great that You can use anyone to speak to us, even our own children. Once You even used a donkey to speak to Balaam. Thanks for sending me a message. I needed to hear it.

Rejoice always; pray without ceasing; in every-

thing give thanks; for this is God's will for you in Christ
Jesus (1 Thess. 5:16–18).

30. AM I A COCONUT?

I have to laugh, Lord, every time I look back to the time my oldest was two years old and terribly frustrated with me because I wouldn't let him do something he dearly wanted to do. He glared at me, put his hands on his hips, and said the worst thing he could think of, "Mommy, you're a . . . you're a . . . you're a coconut!"

Am I a coconut, Lord? Today I sort of feel like some kind of a nut! I'm not sure I'm not losing it!

Trying to juggle my job, my family, my chores, and everything else I need to do sometimes causes me to meet myself coming and going. I don't always remember everything I need to. I don't always get everything done. Once in a while, late at night, I wonder if I'm going to make it through this single-parenting experience. I turn to You and Your Word for reassurance, for guidance, and for hope.

I find them.

The mystery for me is how I can read a verse I've read dozens of times before and have the Holy Spirit bring out new depths and meaning to the words, so that my heart is touched just the way I need. Sometimes I don't even have to be reading the Word for the Holy Spirit to work. Verses I memorized as a little girl are brought to my mind as clearly as if I were reading them.

Your Word feeds my soul, is comforting, reassuring, encouraging, and instructive, as well as timely. I am impressed that I need to find ways of encouraging and motivating my children to read and memorize Your Word, so the Holy Spirit can speak to them the same way He does to me.

No, I'm not a coconut, just one tired mother who needs a bit of reassurance from time to time.

Thank You, Lord, for Your Word.

> All Scripture is inspired by God and profitable for teaching, for reproof, for correction, for training in righteousness; that the man of God may be adequate, equipped for every good work (2 Tim. 3:16–17).

31. THERE'S SOMETHING SPECIAL ABOUT ONE OF THEIR SMILES

I wish we smiled more often, Lord. I've always loved to see my children smile. My favorite pictures of them are the ones where they are smiling or laughing with seemingly total enjoyment.

I find I look for ways to get my children to smile and laugh. I write them little notes in their lunches, send them cartoons, plan special treats, and cook favorite meals. I tell them when I'm proud of choices they've made, when I'm pleased with their behaviors, and when I appreciate favors they do for me. I hug them frequently and remind them daily that I love them. They usually respond to all these things with big smiles and I love it.

Today at dinner we were laughing together about something that had happened and suddenly one of the kids looked at me solemnly and said, "Mommy, I like it when you laugh. You don't laugh very often." I think he was right. I do try to keep a stiff upper lip, and I often force a tight smile when I'd rather cry. But I don't often relax and laugh with easy enjoyment. I never thought that the kids liked to see me smiling and laughing just as much as I like to see them doing that!

Maybe I do take myself, my life, and my responsibilities way too seriously. Maybe I do need to become more human and less of a "mother-machine" doing all of the "right" things. Interesting how once again I am taught from a little child a very deep lesson of life. Is that why You loved the children when You were here? Because they go right through the layers of defenses and touch the issues?

Give me a smile, Lord, and a ready laugh. It will not only do me good, but will help my family as well.

> But Jesus called for them, saying "Permit the children to come to Me, and do not hinder them, for the kingdom of God belongs to such as these. Truly I say to you, whoever does not receive the kingdom of God like a child shall not enter it at all" (Luke 18:16–17).

32. I GUESS I REALLY WAS YELLING

Okay, I was yelling, Lord. There I was in the kitchen, my guests nearby in the living room, and I was glaring at my youngest. I hissed through clenched teeth that he was misbehaving and embarrassing me. Whispering so that my friends wouldn't hear, I laid down the law. Either he straightened up or he would experience the worst possible punishment I could think of.

"Quit yelling at me!" he screamed at me, embarrassing me further, for my guests couldn't help but hear him.

Indignantly, self-righteously, I reminded him that I wasn't yelling, I was whispering.

"It feels like you're yelling!" he responded.

And he was right. Except for the level of the sound of my voice, I was yelling at him.

How often do I fool myself into rationalizing that because I'm not overtly doing something wrong, I needn't worry about the attitude of my heart? Probably more often than I'd care to admit. Keeping a right attitude is so hard, much more difficult than simply behaving correctly.

Lord, forgive not only my wrong actions, but also my wrong attitudes. Give me the wisdom and self-discipline to change my inappropriate attitudes, so that I can become a better woman, mother, and Christian.

> For the good that I wish, I do not do; but I practice the very evil that I do not wish. But if I am doing the very thing I do not wish, I am no longer the one doing it, but sin which dwells in me. I find then the principle that evil is present in me, the one who wishes to do good. . . . Who will set me free from the body of this death? Thanks be to God through Jesus Christ our Lord! So then, on the one hand I myself with my mind am serving the law of God, but on the other, with my flesh the law of sin (Rom. 7:19–25).
>
> If we confess our sins, He is faithful and righteous to forgive us our sins and to cleanse us from all unrighteousness (1 John 1:9).

33. I ALMOST MISSED A MILESTONE

I'm glad You're never too busy for us, Lord! Last night I almost missed a major milestone in the life of one of my kids. He came in while I was preparing dinner, and I paid very little attention while he told me about his day. He was angry at his teacher for saying that he wasn't trying hard to get his school work right. "I do try, as hard as I can, Mom," he insisted. He described his feelings about being accused falsely and said that he had gone up to the teacher after class and told her how he felt. If I had paid attention, I would have been amazed at this change in a boy who usually either withdrew into himself or smashed things when he was angry! Success, finally, after several years of trying to teach him to verbalize his anger and to attempt to resolve conflicts verbally! But I wasn't paying attention, and he finished his story and went outside to play.

Hours later, as I was preparing for bed, I was reminded of what I had only half heard. I was amazed! I almost went to wake my son and to congratulate him, but I waited until this morning.

When I started telling my son how proud I was of him for finally starting to verbalize anger and to seek resolution, he looked up at me shyly and said, "Guess I'm growing up, huh?" Guess so.

How special that the Holy Spirit can get through to even the busiest of us and remind us of what we need to remember! How terrific that You care enough about the little things to remind us!

Lord, make me more aware of the real issues in our family (loving, sharing, growing) and less concerned with the tasks (cooking, cleaning, shopping). Don't let me miss these milestones in our family life.

And, Lord, make me aware of the milestones in my own life. I think this moment of awareness is one.
Thanks.

> But the Helper, the Holy Spirit, whom the Father will send in My name, He will teach you all things, and bring to your remembrance all that I said to you (John 14:26).

34. I HATE IT WHEN KIDS LIE

Lying is such an ugly thing, Lord. It destroys trust and damages relationships. I truly hate it when someone lies to me, and I hate it more than ever if it is one of my kids who is lying.

Sometimes they don't mean to lie at the time, they just say they'll do something (chores, errands, homework) and then don't keep their word. But that's a form of lying. Sometimes they're afraid of the consequences of telling the truth. They know they'll be found out eventually, but better later than now. Sometimes they don't know the answer to what I ask and, rather than finding out, they make up an answer. Last week one said, "I left my jacket at Billy's house," when he didn't know where the jacket actually was! Sometimes they lie to get something else they want— "Dad said we could if you agreed, Mom," when they haven't yet talked to Dad.

So many excuses for, and ways of, lying. Am I guilty also, Lord? Is my walk open and honest? Do I tell the truth lovingly, or shade the truth, fib, or use "little white lies"? Yes, Lord, sometimes I lie, in one way or another. I need to face the truth and strive to live an honest life as not only an example to my children, but also as an example of what a believer should be.

How easy it is to be tempted by the father of lies, Satan, and to slide into a lifestyle of lying. Here I was so angry with the children when my own life needed some work.

> Therefore, laying aside falsehood, speak truth, each one of you, with his neighbor, for we are members of one another (Eph. 4:25).
>
> Do not lie to one another, since you laid aside the old self with its evil practices, and have put on the new self who is being renewed to a true knowledge according to the image of the One who created him (Col. 3:9–10).

Challenges

35. I FIND THAT SAYING "NO" IS SOMETIMES HARD

Oh, Lord! My calendar is too full! I know how it got that way. I just find it hard to say "no" sometimes. If someone needs a favor, they know to ask me because the odds are very good that I'll say, "yes." So, here I am this week, baking six pies for the school bake sale, watching a friend's two babies all day Saturday, substitute teaching a Sunday school class, and making play costumes, for not only my two children, but three of the other children in the play.

That's crazy! I have enough to do with my regular routine. Sure, I can sometimes add a couple of things, but I should never get as over-committed as I frequently do!

I've looked at why it's hard for me to say "no," Lord, and I think I know what it is. I want people to like me and to think well of me. I want approval, and somewhere I've decided that approval comes when I say "yes." Approval is nice, but I've gotten in the habit of giving the "getting of approval" more priority than taking care of the real priorities in my life. The other day when I was making a special cake for a friend, one of the kids complained, "Mom you're always so busy doing things for other people you don't have time to do things for us!" Not totally true, but true enough.

I'm going to start making better choices for committing my time and energies. I want to learn to say "no" when appropriate. I need to say "yes" more to my family.

Give me the wisdom I need, Lord, to recognize what my choices should be.

> . . . therefore be shrewd as serpents, and innocent as doves (Matt. 10:16b).
> But if anyone does not provide for his own, and

especially for those of his household, he has denied the faith, and is worse than an unbeliever (1 Tim. 5:8).

36. THIS IS WAR!

Life has many faces, Lord. At times it is a ball, at times a joy, or a blast, or a challenge, pain, jungle, or war. Yes, an all-out war. That is a perfect description of my life this week. I feel as if I'm under attack from all sides. My defenses are up, and I'm ready to fight back at the slightest hint of an offensive move.

I have a whole defense strategy in place, for all the good it does me, and I hate how I'm behaving. I'm withholding information, being suspicious, putting the worst possible connotation on the words and actions of others. I am critical, arbitrary, controlling, and irritable. All because I've been hurt by one friend, disappointed by another, resisted by the kids, and attacked by Satan.

Why do I try to cope with weeks like this on my own strength with such ineffective weapons? I waste not only the time and energy, but also opportunities which come my way because I'm too busy fighting real (and imagined) enemies.

There is a better way.

You said to love my enemies. You said to treat them kindly. To forgive, then forgive again. You said You'd take care of ensuring that justice is served.

My job is to suit up with the proper and very effective armor You provide, so I can win in a much bigger war—one with eternal consequences.

Give me strength. Give me the armor. Give me the victory. Please.

Finally, be strong in the Lord, and in the strength of His might. Put on the full armor of God, that you may be able to stand firm against the schemes of the devil. For our struggle is not against flesh and blood, but against the rulers, against the powers, against the world forces of this darkness, against the spiritual forces of wickedness in the heavenly places. Therefore, take up the full armor of God, that you may be able to resist in the evil day, and having done everything, to stand firm. Stand firm therefore, having girded your loins with truth, and having put on the breastplate of righteousness, and having shod your feet with the preparation of the gospel of peace; in addition to all, taking up the shield of faith with which you will be able to extinguish all the flaming missiles of the evil one. And take the helmet of salvation, and the sword of the Spirit, which is the Word of God (Eph. 6:10–18).

37. I TRY TO FACE ONLY ONE DAY AT A TIME

I like those bumper stickers, Lord, which say "One Day At A Time." Whenever I'm driving and see one, I smile, thinking that the person in the other car is struggling just as I do. We may have different problems and challenges, but we have both learned that the only way to survive is to face one day at a time. Sometimes I wave at the other driver and give him or her a big smile. They probably think I'm crazy, but I think everyone can use an extra, unexpected smile just about any time.

I wonder how many people there are in the world, or even just in my neighborhood, who are hanging on by their proverbial fingernails and trying to cope, just one day at a time. I bet, if people were honest, that most of them are doing that to some degree.

Living one day at a time has its advantages. The past is over, and the future isn't here yet. I only have to cope with today's choices, today's decisions, and today's disappointments. I can't borrow from tomorrow's joys, or sorrows. They are reserved for me for tomorrow. That's nice.

You've told us to only live one day at a time and that's good advice. You know that we only have strength for one day, so only give us what we can handle. Give me strength for today, and the reminders I need to let tomorrow take care of itself.

> Come now, you who say, "Today or tomorrow, we shall go to such and such a city, and spend a year there and engage in business and make a profit." Yet you do not know what your life will be like tomorrow. You are just a vapor that appears for a little while and then vanishes away. Instead, you ought to say, "If the Lord wills, we shall live and also do this or that" (James 4:13–15).

38. I TRY TO BE A GOOD DISCIPLINARIAN, BUT . . .

It's hard to have to discipline the kids, Lord. I never would have believed it when I was a child, but now I'm sure that it's harder on the parent than on the kids.

I want to teach the children to follow rules, to respect authority, and to behave properly. I want them to learn that there are adverse consequences for not doing these

70

things. So, I set rules, establish consequences, and enforce them both.

On the other hand, I don't want to be a tyrant, or unreasonable. I want to be fair. And I don't want to crush the spirits of the children. How do I find the balance?

When one of the boys looks up at me with tears in his eyes, bottom lip quivering, I'm ready to cave in, dismiss the offense, and hug him. I know I can't do that, or he'd never learn. So, I don't. I do the "right" thing and feel like a meanie. I do, however, seem to find new ways to assure the kids that I love them even when I'm being firm.

Sometimes when the consequences are particularly significant, my heart aches for the culprit. I wish he hadn't broken the rules so he wouldn't have to suffer.

I'm sure You know what I mean, Lord. Not only because you know my heart, but also because You have rules too, and sometimes I find myself suffering the consequences of breaking the rules. When I hurt because of my own foolishness, I'm sure that it hurts Your own heart. Yet, You let me take the consequences because You want me to learn, because You love me.

Help me to love my children enough to be a good disciplinarian.

He who spares his rod hates his son, but he who loves him disciplines him diligently (Prov. 13:24).

Furthermore, we had earthly fathers to discipline us, and we respected them; shall we not much rather be subject to the Father of spirits, and live? For they disciplined us for a short time as seemed best to them, but He disciplines us for our good, that we may share His holiness. All discipline for the moment seems not to be joyful, but sorrowful; yet to those who have been trained by it, afterwards it yields the peaceful fruit of righteousness (Heb. 12:9–11).

39. THERE'S NEVER ENOUGH MONEY

On television tonight a famous announcer was telling people to be sure and enter the Publisher's Clearinghouse Sweepstakes. The grand prize was millions of dollars.

I could use even one million dollars, Lord. If I had a million dollars, I would give a lot of it away. I'd support missionaries, help the homeless, build churches in faraway lands. I'd pay off all our debts, and set up trust funds for the kids. I could do grand things with that prize money.

But I'll never win the sweepstakes; I don't even bother returning those entry blanks. So much for short-lived dreams of being rich.

But I just realized that I don't have to give up the essence of the dreams. I may not have millions to give, but I can give what I have. I can support missionaries by praying regularly for them and their work. I can write them letters to keep them aware that they are not forgotten. I can send a small donation. I can help the homeless by giving outgrown clothes to the shelter, by donating time to help serve at special times of the year when the community provides a big meal (Thanksgiving, Christmas). I can give a small donation. There's an orphanage nearby where I can give my time to read to or play with the children, and rest homes where elderly people sit alone and forgotten. Jails and prisons are filled with lost people who need to know of Your love.

I feel as if I've caught a new vision. I remember a saying I heard long ago: "Between the big things we cannot do, and the little things we won't do, most of us do nothing."

I may not have a lot of money, but I have a lot to give. Help me to not do nothing.

And He looked up and saw the rich putting their gifts into the treasury. And He saw a certain poor widow putting in two small copper coins. And He said, "Truly I say to you, this poor widow put in more than all of them; for they all out of their surplus put into the offering; but she out of her poverty put in all that she had to live on" (Luke 21:1–4).

40. IT WAS ONE OF THOSE DAYS

It started out to be one of those days, Lord. You know the kind, the ones when the best thing you could do is crawl back into bed and hide under the covers, until the next morning when you can just start over. Unfortunately, on *those* kind of days, you usually can't run away and hide because you just have too much to do.

By ten o'clock this morning we had three arguments, two broken glasses, a torn shirt, a stopped-up sink, a recalcitrant lawnmower which refused to start, and we were no longer speaking to each other. I'm afraid we were reduced to yelling at each other. The feelings within the family weren't very nice. What I wanted to do was walk out the front door, climb into the car, drive off, and never come back.

Instead, I brewed a cup of tea and went out onto the patio to calm down and regain my sanity. I prayed and asked You for guidance. You gave me a good idea. I could put a stop to the downward spiraling of the day. I called the kids out and suggested that we could probably turn the day around, if we all would work at it. They agreed.

So, we made a list of what to accomplish and then

each of us added something which we would like to do for fun. We organized the work first and saved the fun things for last as rewards. Knowing that we were soon going to be doing fun things helped us get the work done more quickly and cheerfully.

After the work, we enjoyed the fun things on our list.

Thank You, Lord, for helping us turn one of *those* (bad) days into one of *those* (good) days.

> As thy days, so shall thy strength be (Deut. 33:25 KJV).

41. WE LOVE TO SHARE OUR HOME

It's fun to have guests in our home. We seem to volunteer almost every time our church asks people to open their homes. We've had singing group members, visiting missionaries, speakers, and once we had even a whole single-parent family for a weekend. There's something festive about getting out the sleeping bags for the kids and putting out fresh towels for the guests. I like getting up early to prepare a special breakfast.

Our home isn't fancy. In fact, it's quite small, but somehow the guests don't seem to mind.

At night over dinner, and afterwards, the visitors tell their stories. How they got started in their careers/ministries, what things You are doing in their lives, their hopes and dreams. I feel my little world expanding as I listen. My faith is strengthened as I hear them sing Your praises. My own hopes and dreams are rekindled.

I think these times are good for the children too. They

get to hear testimonies of how You work in other people's lives. Also, I love to hear one of the kids chime in with a story about when You answered a prayer.

In sharing, we all grow.

Keep on bringing visitors to our home, Lord.

> Let love of the brethren continue. Do not neglect to show hospitality to strangers, for by this some have entertained angels without knowing it (Heb. 13:1–2).

42. WE ARE LEARNING FORGIVENESS

I think we are learning, Lord, but forgiveness doesn't come easy. I'm not sure why, but it seems as if forgiving within the family is sometimes harder than forgiving friends. But I am seeing progress in all of us as we work through the disappointments, the conflicts, and the hurts of family life.

One of the kids apologized to the other today without any coaching from me and his apology was graciously accepted. That's progress, Lord! I've seen signs of real forgiveness in the kids as they tell about their relationships with friends. It's as if they're learning that loving is more important than hating, and that they have a choice between staying angry and hurt or releasing these feelings through forgiveness.

I've seen myself becoming more understanding and less ready to read wrong motives into the kids' actions. When one of the kids tracked mud across my newly waxed floor, my instinctive response was, ''If you really loved me, you'd never track mud on my floor! You just proved you don't care about me!" But, before I said anything, I realized that love (or the lack thereof) had nothing to do with a young boy's not realizing he was tracking mud. So, I simply pointed out that there was now mud on the floor and asked him to please clean it up. In a way, it was forgiveness because I chose not to let his thoughtlessness or his actions hurt me. I forgave his shortcomings and loved him.

You sent your Son to die so that we could be forgiven for our sins. We haven't learned to always be forgiving, but thanks to your loving example and the power of your Spirit, we're on our way.

> Then Peter came and said to Him, "Lord, how often shall my brother sin against me and I forgive him? Up to seven times?" Jesus said to him, "I do not say to you, up to seven times, but up to seventy times seven" (Matt. 18:21–22).
> And do not grieve the Holy Spirit of God, by whom you were sealed for the day of redemption. Let all bitterness and wrath and anger and clamor and slander be put away from you, along with all malice. And be kind to one another, tender-hearted, forgiving each other, just as God in Christ also has forgiven you (Eph. 4:30–32).

43. I DIDN'T WANT TO GET UP TODAY

When I woke up today I wondered what it would be like to be able to just stay in bed all day and be waited on hand and foot. Breakfast in bed, a favorite book, a cup of hot tea to sip. My type of music coming from the radio and no one, but no one, calling "Mommy, Mommy" for at least eight hours. Such are the dreams of a very tired mommy who at times feels as if she is always taking care of others.

Actually I do enjoy being needed by the kids. I like organizing schedules and budgets, planning the meals, and doing the laundry. I feel so efficient. And I like knowing that they're eating nutritiously and wearing clean clothes. So, why do I sometimes want to play hooky from my job as mother? I guess I just get tired. That's okay. As long as I recognize that it's not a permanent feeling.

You know what it's like being a "giver," a person who does for others. When You were here on earth, everywhere You went people came looking for miracles, for wisdom, for help. If people couldn't get to You one way, they tried another, like the men who lowered a friend to You through a hole in the roof! Did You ever get tired of the people, of the constant demands on You? Did You ever dream of lying abed and being taken care of?

Even if You did, You kept on giving and going for others. So, remembering Your example, I did get up today and did my job. It was okay!

> And calling them to Himself, Jesus said to them, "You know that those who are recognized as rulers of the Gentiles lord it over them; and their great men exercise authority over them. But it is not so among you, but whoever wishes to become great among you shall be your servant; and whoever wishes to be first among you shall be slave of all. For even the Son of Man did not come to be served, but to serve, and to give His life a ransom for many" (Mark 10:42–45).

44. I DON'T THINK I'M SMART ENOUGH

Sometimes I wish You'd give me a parenting manual, guaranteed to produce well-balanced children who will grow up into mature, wise, and kind adults. There are too many options, too many possibilities, and I don't know the best ones to choose.

I think back to the "mistakes" I used to think my parents made, and realize that they were trying their best to do the right things with their children and to avoid "mistakes" their own parents had made. So, here I am, doing my best to not make "mistakes," and I'm not sure I'd recognize a mistake if I saw one!

Sometimes at night after the kids have gone to sleep, I lie awake wondering if I'm doing all I need to be doing to teach my children everything they need to know. There have been nights when You've given me ideas about how I could do better, and I appreciate all Your help. But, Lord, I really don't feel smart enough or wise enough to do this job.

Each morning as I pray, I ask for wisdom and guidance. I believe that You are providing them, since You promised You would. Help me be ever sensitive to Your leading, so I don't have to be smart enough, just willing enough to follow.

Trust in the Lord with all your heart, and do not lean on your own understanding. In all your ways acknowledge Him, and He will make your paths straight. Do not be wise in your own eyes (Prov. 3:5–7a).

But if any of you lacks wisdom, let him ask of God, who gives to all men generously and without reproach, and it will be given to him. But let him ask in faith without any doubting, for the one who doubts is like the surf of the sea driven and tossed by the wind. For let not that man expect that he will receive anything from the Lord, being a double-minded man, unstable in all his ways (James 1:5–8).

Hope

45. I'M DOING OKAY

I'm doing fine, Lord. I really am. Sitting here tonight on the floor in front of the fire in the fireplace, I've been thinking about our family. We've been through a lot.

The breakup of our original family was hard, but we've survived. We moved, and as I look around the room I can see that we've made our new house into a comfortable home. It looks like us, mostly straightened, but not perfect. Favorite pictures and knickknacks fill in the spaces.

We've made new friends, many are single-parent families like us. We get together, in what turns out to sometimes be rowdy bunches, to laugh and play in the park or at the beach.

We've restyled our habits to fit our reduced budget, but we've still found ways to squeeze in a few frills and fun expenses.

We have some new house rules and chores, not all of which are fun, but on the whole we pull together and get the jobs done.

I've had to learn a few new roles myself which, at first, were uncomfortable—like being the disciplinarian, taking care of the car maintenance, and making home repairs. But even these roles are less strange to me now and manageable.

I've rescheduled my own chores to ensure that I have some quality time with the kids each evening, and our family is closer now than before.

I read the Bible with the children, and we pray together each night. They're learning about You.

I didn't plan to be a single parent, but with Your help, I'm doing okay! Thanks, Lord.

Therefore, do not throw away your confidence,

which has a great reward. For you have need of endurance, so that when you have done the will of God, you may receive what was promised. For yet in a very little while, He who is coming will come, and will not delay. But My righteous one shall live by faith; and if he shrinks back, My soul has no pleasure in him. But we are not of those who shrink back to destruction, but of those who have faith to the preserving of the soul (Heb. 10:35–39).

46. WILL THEY REALLY STAY ON THE RIGHT PATH?

Sometimes I worry, Lord. Will my children really continue their walk with You as they grow up? There are so many pressures on them to go the way of the world.

We were talking the other day about drugs in school. I asked the kids what they would do if they saw someone selling drugs at school. "Nothing," was the response from my oldest son. "Almost everybody is either selling or buying drugs!" And Lord, we're talking about sixth graders. Life is different today than when I grew up. We didn't have to make choices about drugs when I was in grade school. And attitudes in the world are more accepting of immorality and dishonesty. What chance do children have of growing up living a pure, Christian life?

The truth is, they don't have a chance at all! If it weren't for Your Holy Spirit's influence and protection, we'd all be living the world's way. The challenge for me is to make my kids familiar with Scripture while they're young, to teach them Your way of living, and to make sure my own walk is close to You and a model to follow.

You've promised that if I'm faithful in doing my part to teach and train my children, they will follow Your way in the end. I will put even more effort into doing my job, and the most effort into trusting You to do Yours.

Train up a child in the way he should go, even when he is old he will not depart from it (Prov. 22:6).

47. THE CHURCH WAS HELPFUL THIS WEEK

I'm very glad for our church, Lord. The staff is genuinely concerned for people, and the programs seem geared directly to meet needs. This week one of my needs was met and I'm thankful.

There was a workshop on Saturday on single parenting. I went because I'm a single parent, and I'd feel guilty not going to find out how to be a better mom. I sort of went to find out what all I was doing wrong. The lecturer was great, amusing but with very practical ideas. The best value was the small group discussions where we interacted with the material and shared our own experiences.

I was amazed to hear people expressing my own thoughts and fears. Some, I'd never shared with anyone but You for fear of people's reactions. Saturday, I found out I'm not the only parent who sometimes wants to resign, walk out, or run away! I'm not alone in sometimes hating my role as a parent. I discovered that most parents have times when they'd rather not be one.

What a freeing discovery!

I took lots of notes about better ways to communicate with children, tactics for handling discipline, and methods for avoiding power plays. I'm kind of excited to start practicing new skills. I think I'll write the pastor a little note and let him know that he's doing something helpful. I think he'd like to know how he (and the church) helped me this week.

> I thank my God always, making mention of you in my prayers, because I hear of your love, and of the faith which you have toward the Lord Jesus, and toward all the saints; and I pray that the fellowship of your faith may become effective through the knowledge of every good thing which is in you for Christ's sake. For I have come to have much joy and comfort in your love, because the hearts of the saints have been refreshed through you, brother (Philemon 1:4–7).

48. MY FAITH IS STRONG

My faith grew today, Lord. We had a missionary speaker at church, and her stories of Your miraculous care were so inspiring. I caught myself wishing I could witness miracles like hers. Then she concluded by reminding us that You are the God of Abraham, Isaac and Jacob, of creation, of Calvary, and of today!

You are the same God everywhere. And the miracles we experience are in direct relationship to our needs and our awareness of You. If a missionary's story of Your help seems more dramatic than mine, that's because her need was probably more urgent. I honestly haven't needed You to recently close a jaguar's mouth so he wouldn't eat me. She did. I haven't needed You to drop a doctor in my front yard by downing his small plane (safely) because my doctor is either available or has another doctor covering for him.

She had no way to get a doctor for that dying child. She needed a big miracle.

But I have had needs and these You met. Financial needs. Support needs. Wisdom needs. And strength needs. You've closed the mouth of those who would wound me with words. You have sent angels to protect me and my children as we travel here and there on busy freeways, running errands. Whatever I've needed, You have provided, even if it wasn't all I *wanted*! I confess, some of my wants are a bit fanciful and unnecessary. But tonight, remembering all You have done, I feel so comforted, so confident that I needn't worry. Whatever comes, You can handle it.

Now, about this tall, dark, and handsome doctor I'd like You to drop at my front door. . . Oh well, it was just a fantasy!

> Now faith is the assurance of things hoped for, the conviction of things not seen. For by it the men of old gained approval. By faith we understand that the worlds were prepared by the word of God, so that what is seen was not made out of things which are visible. . . . And without faith it is impossible to please Him, for he who comes to God must believe that He is, and that He is a rewarder of those who seek Him (Heb. 11:1–3,6).

49. MY FRIENDS HELP A LOT

I have such neat friends, Lord. I called up a couple of them today and suggested that we get together because I said, "I need a hug."

They rose to the challenge and "hugged" me in so

many ways. One came over and shooed me out of the kitchen, so she could prepare supper for all of us. The other brought a favorite table game which kept all of the children occupied, happy, and relatively quiet for nearly two hours. We three adults were able to sit in the living room with tall glasses of iced tea and our feet propped up on the coffee table and just relax.

We talked. We laughed. We even giggled a little. It was just what I needed to feel perked up and revived. I'm ready for the rest of the week now!

I like this gift You give us called "friendships." Good times are more fun when shared with friends. And the tough times are easier when shared. Friends are wonderful.

Friends can give me a different perspective when I'm all tangled up in a problem.

Friends can give a hand when the task is too big for one person.

Friends at least listen to my side of the story.

Friends appreciate me.

Friends encourage me to keep on trying when all I want to do is quit.

Friends give me nudges when inertia sets in, and I can't get started on the things I need to do.

Friends remind me of Your power when I've forgotten who the source is.

Friends . . . well, friends, are totally necessary for life.

Thank You, God, for friends.

Bear one another's burdens, and thus fulfill the law of Christ (Gal. 6:2).

Since you have in obedience to the truth purified your souls for a sincere love of the brethren, fervently love one another from the heart (1 Peter 1:22).

Joy

50. GROWING UP IS EXCITING

I would never want to be twelve again, Lord. In fact, I'd just as soon never be sixteen, twenty, or even twenty-five again! There's a lot to be said for growing up.

Kids know this. They're always eager to have birthdays and to check their heights against the marks on the kitchen doorway where we've indicated their growth. They like checking to see if they can run faster or jump higher than before, and they love showing off what they've learned.

Me too. I'm always setting goals for myself, achievement goals, learning goals, or skill goals. Then I set out to reach those goals. I love to note my progress, to measure myself against the identified benchmarks, and to celebrate the end results. It's great to look back over the years of my life and note the significant areas of growth.

I think one of the greatest truths is that we're never all grown up and finished. As long as we're alive, we can keep stretching and growing. The other day I heard of a ninety-three-year-old woman who took her first training parachute jump out of an airplane! That's pretty adventuresome! I may not ever jump out of an airplane, but I do hope that when I'm ninety-three, I'm still learning and trying new things.

One area I want to always work on is deepening my personal relationship with You, Lord. I want to get to know You so well and spend so much time with You that people will begin to see You in me and to say I act like You.

That's one of my goals, the most important one.

When I was a child, I used to speak as a child, think as a child, reason as a child; when I became a man, I did away with childish things (1 Cor. 13:11).

For whom He foreknew, He also predestined to become conformed to the image of His Son, that He might be the first-born among many brethren (Rom. 8:29).

51. I LOVE GETTING GOOD NEWS

Today was my day for good news, Lord. I was told at work that I'm getting a promotion. I received my (small, but welcome) income tax refund check. I got a letter from a friend back East who said she was coming to visit. And both kids brought home school papers with good grades! Wow!

I almost wished that I'd gotten these each on different days because getting good news is such a great experience it makes my whole day. I could have had several great days with the news I received today!

There is actually good news every day, if I'd take time to recognize it, isn't there, Lord? The good news is . . .

I'm alive.

I'm healthy.

I'm warm, fed, and housed comfortably.

I have a great family.

I have friends who love me.

I have a church which meets my spiritual needs, and many other needs also.

I have a job.

I live in a free country.

I can worship as I choose.

You love me.

You have given me eternal life.

You will supply my need.

You will provide wisdom if asked.

You are my Lord, my Savior, my King, and my Father.

Thank You, Lord, for all the terrific news, each and every day.

> Like cold water to a weary soul, so is good news from a distant land (Prov. 25:25).
>
> See how great a love the Father has bestowed upon us, that we should be called children of God; and such we are. For this reason the world does not know us, because it did not know Him. Beloved, now we are children of God, and it has not appeared as yet what we shall be. We know that, when He appears, we shall be like Him, because we shall see Him just as He is (1 John 3:1–2).

52. MY JOY IS FULL

I woke up singing this morning, Lord. I had slept well and was refreshed. I enjoyed those few minutes of puttering around alone in the kitchen before the kids got up. The sky was beautiful as I took time to go outside and watch the sunrise. I felt like playing Julie Andrews and twirling down a grassy hillside singing "The Sound of Music."

During breakfast we listened to a great Bible teacher on the radio who reminded us that we serve a tremendous God. He read one of David's Psalms which magnified Your name, and I felt uplifted with each verse.

As I drove to work, I felt so conscious of Your love and grace towards me. I am humbled when I remember how I so often let You down. How do You ever put up with us human beings? We adults act like children a lot of the time!

It is such a privilege to have a personal relationship with You, Lord. So many people in the world don't know You, don't pray to You, don't come to You for comfort. What terrible lives they must lead! I can't even imagine not having You in my life.

Thank You for the promise that You will never leave me nor forsake me. Thank You for listening to me, for answering my prayers. Thank You for caring not only for my soul, but for my joy also.

> If you keep My commandments, you will abide in My love; just as I have kept My Father's commandments, and abide in His love. These things I have spoken to you, that My joy may be in you, and that your joy may be made full (John 15:10–11).

53. YOU PRAYED FOR ME

It feels special to have someone pray for me, Lord.

Today when I called the pastor to ask for prayer, he immediately said, "Okay, let's pray now." And we did, right over the telephone. He thanked You for me and for the way I try to live for You. He brought my request to You and added his own request on my behalf. I felt hugged, warmed, appreciated, and supported.

It's such a special feeling to join with friends and talk together with You. It seems so intimate, as if for a moment the whirl of the world has stopped and we are calmed by You. There's a unique sense of connectedness. I guess there's a part of me that feels as if maybe You'll listen and be more likely to answer if several of us are praying to You. But I also think that praying for someone is another way of saying, "I care."

Maybe that's why I love reading John 17. That was one of Your prayers and You prayed for me!

If God will listen to anyone, He'll listen to You, and You prayed for me! How caring. How intimate. How wonderful. How awesome! And Hebrews tells us that as our High Priest, You are forever interceding on our behalf with the Father.

What a thought!

Thank You, Lord, for praying for me.

> I ask on their behalf; I do not ask on behalf of the world, but of those whom Thou has given Me; for they are Thine; and all things that are Mine are Thine, and Thine are Mine; and I have been glorified in them. And I am no more in the world; and yet they themselves are in the world, and I come to Thee. Holy Father, keep them in Thy name, the name which Thou has given Me, that they may be one, even as We are. While I was with them, I was keeping them in Thy name which Thou hast given Me; and I guarded them, and not one of them perished but the son of perdition, that the Scripture might be fulfilled. But now I come to Thee; and these things I speak in the world, that they may have My joy made full in themselves. I have given them Thy word; and the world has hated them, because they are not of the world, even as I am not of the world. I do not ask Thee to take them out of the world, but to keep them from the evil one (John 17:9–15).